The Impossible Rescue

by Mark Spann
illustrated by Paul Bachem

MODERN CURRICULUM PRESS
Pearson Learning Group

A freight train pulled out of a snowy train yard on a cold night in February, 1996. Everything seemed fine. Six locomotives pulled the train, which had almost ninety freight cars.

The train moved faster. It rolled down a steep hill toward St. Paul, Minnesota. Something was wrong. When the engineer tried to slow the train, nothing happened. The brakes didn't work!

The train sped out of control. The engineer grabbed his radio. He dispatched a warning to the train yard in St. Paul.

No one at the train yard was very worried. Everything would be fine as long as the train stayed on the track. It would slow down when it started up the next hill. It would soon coast to a stop.

They didn't know that something else was wrong.

Some track switches were in the wrong position. Suddenly the runaway train barreled onto the wrong track. Now it was headed right for the train yard in St. Paul!

Other locomotives, called haulers, were parked on the same track in front of the yard office. If the runaway train crashed into these locomotives, the office would also be wrecked.

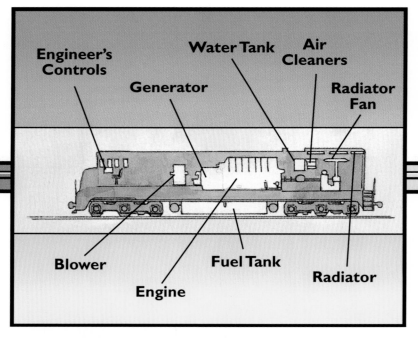

Cutaway Diagram of Diesel Electric Locomotive

Inside the yard office, Richard Vitek, an engineer, was getting ready to work on another train. He didn't know about the runaway train.

Richard stepped out of the office. He couldn't believe what he saw. The huge headlight of a train was heading right for the haulers. And right for him! He jumped back into the office just as the runaway train plowed into the train yard. It knocked the other cars off the track as if they were toys. The crash was bone-shattering.

Freight cars jumped the track and piled up behind the locomotives. Pieces of metal and wood flew everywhere.

Ambulances and fire trucks were dispatched to the train yard. The rescuers found eight people who were injured and needed to go to a hospital. One of them told the rescuers that Richard was missing.

"He may be under the wreckage," someone said. But the office was just a huge pile of wood and twisted metal. One locomotive and a freight car full of grain lay on top of it.

Firefighters searched through the wreckage. They had to move slowly and carefully. The debris could fall and crush Richard.

"Is anyone there?" the firefighters called out. At first they didn't hear anyone. Then one of the firefighters heard a weak voice.

"I'm here."

Where was it coming from?

"I'm down here," the voice repeated. Rescuers searched with their flashlights. Finally, they spotted one of Richard's shoes.

Richard was lying on his stomach. He was trapped
in a shallow hole. Fuel seeped from the wrecked
locomotive and formed a puddle in front of him. The
fumes stung his eyes and face.

The freight car full of grain was leaking too. The trapped man had to push the grain away from his face so that he could breathe. But it was hard work. One of his arms was pinned underneath him.

A firefighter found a place to crawl under the wreckage. He kept telling Richard they would get him out.

But could they?

The rescuers used jacks to raise some of the wreckage so Richard could breathe more easily. But they couldn't lift the freight cars and the locomotive. And they couldn't move the wreckage. If they did, it might fall and crush the man.

How could they get him out? It seemed impossible.

It took them a long time to decide what to try. Richard must have wondered if he would ever see his family again.

Firefighters carry special tools for rescuing people. But they couldn't use any of them now. They couldn't use electrical tools because a spark might start a fire. And they couldn't lift the heavy wreckage enough to pull Richard out.

One of the firefighters had an idea. They could use special, air-powered chisels.

One of the firefighters crawled back into the hole. He used the chisel to break up the frozen ground. The plan was to make a shallow hole next to Richard. He would have to slide into it. Then the rescuers could pull him out.

It would take a long time to dig the hole. Both Richard and the firefighter would be in danger the whole time.

Richard was afraid they couldn't save him. But the rescuers wouldn't give up. "We're going to get you out of here," they told him.

Richard was getting very tired. He had a hard time keeping the grain away from his face. And it was getting harder to hold himself up and away from the puddle of fuel.

The firefighters took turns digging. They worked for almost three hours. Finally, the hole was big enough. Richard inched over and slipped into it. "Pull me out now," he told his rescuers.

One of the firefighters grabbed Richard's coat. Others grabbed the firefighter's ankles. They pulled as hard as they could. Slowly the firefighter slid from under the pile of rubble. He was still holding onto Richard. After a few more pulls, Richard was freed.

The firefighters put Richard on a stretcher and some paramedics examined him. He had bruises on his arms and face. His face was red and raw from the diesel fuel. He also had some pulled muscles. But he felt lucky to be alive and happy that the heroic rescuers hadn't given up.

An ambulance took him to a hospital.

Firefighters and other rescue workers are trained to perform heroic rescues. They have many practice drills to be sure they are ready for a real emergency like the one that happened that night in 1996.

But what makes these people truly heroic is their strong desire to help people. Richard Vitek would certainly agree.